LATIN AMERICA'S
URBAN EXPERIENCE

Latin America's Urban Experience
How markets help developing countries
cope with government dysfunction

Scott Beyer

October 2023

ISBN: 978-1-934276-53-2

Pacific Research Institute
P.O. Box 60485
Pasadena, CA 91116

www.pacificresearch.org
Nothing contained in this report is to be construed as necessarily reflecting
the views of the Pacific Research Institute or as an attempt to thwart or aid
the passage of any legislation. The views expressed remain solely the authors'.
They are not endorsed by any of the authors' past or present affiliations.

LATIN AMERICA'S URBAN EXPERIENCE

HOW MARKETS HELP DEVELOPING COUNTRIES COPE WITH GOVERNMENT DYSFUNCTION

By Scott Beyer

VOLUME FOUR

PRI PACIFIC RESEARCH INSTITUTE

Foreword by Steven Greenhut

Years ago, I was moved by a news article about a horrific shanty-town in sub-Saharan Africa that was transformed into a tolerably decent place after the authorities found a way to provide title to owners of these shacks. After the residents had secure ownership in their properties, they began to upgrade them – sometimes with the help of microloans. The lesson was not that shantytowns are a great idea, but that a market mechanism (property ownership) could help make them much better than they were before. As I recall, the new owners were then able to pool their resources and build a much-needed community property: sanitary restrooms.

In developing countries where many governments are fundamentally corrupt or dysfunctional, market approaches become a necessary end run around official channels. The Free Cities Center featured an in-depth look at Special Economic Zones (SEZs), which are essentially private cities that bypass the usual regulatory morass. Their necessity might not be ideal, but they are a testament to the creative energies of people who are stymied by their own governments. We even see examples in wealthy California, where investors created a quasi-private agency to fund the construction of Orange County toll roads because the state refused to build desperately needed traffic lanes.

We asked Scott Beyer, editor of the *Market Urbanism Report,* to draw on his extensive Latin American travels to see if there are any lessons that Americans can learn. Of course, Beyer isn't suggesting that California abandon all of its regulations or endorse the construction of favelas or shantytowns. Instead, he's providing insight into how even the poorest residents of some of the world's poorest nations have been able to improve their lot by using their own ingenuity – typically in a way that dodges the obstacles their own governments put in their way. Given the freedom, people across the globe will figure out ways to solve their most-pressing problems. Governments often just get in the way, and it can become nearly impossible to streamline encrusted and ill-functioning bureaucracies.

The Free Cities Center's mission is to promote out-of-the-box, market-based thinking to help California and other states fix their intractable problems. All such fixes must come in a way that is appropriate to their respective societies. For instance, we wouldn't suggest that California embrace the kind of chaotic private transportation options one might find in Nicaragua, but we do believe that big, generally affluent cities such as Los Angeles or Seattle should loosen up their rules and allow modern, convenient private transit alternatives to pop up and serve those cities' residents. Even though Latin America's experience won't translate directly to the United States, it's our goal to provide readers with insight into how markets function in other countries. Reducing government's vise grip has improved conditions in the Global South – and it will likewise improve conditions in the wealthier north, often in ways we have yet to envision.

Introduction

Much of my adult life has been spent traveling. Long curious about cities, I lived throughout my twenties in many U.S. ones. After building a journalism career — which allowed for remote work — I spent my early thirties (2015-18) traveling America, as part of a formal project to cover U.S. urban issues.

Now I've taken this act overseas. I'm currently on a 1.5-year tour of the Global South.[1]

"Global South" is a term used somewhat informally to reference the Southern Hemisphere and the developing world. It is used to distinguish from wealthy "Western" societies such as the United States, Canada, Australia and Europe.

My trip began in July 2022, with a plan to spend six months each in Latin America, Africa and Asia.

I viewed this trip as the next step in my education on cities. The Global South deals with very different urban issues — and in some ways feels more relevant right now — than the West. Its population is exploding, with all 20 of the world's fastest-growing cities based in Africa or Asia.[2] More importantly, this population growth has an urban bent; because rural living in the

Global South remains tough, people flood into urban centers. So for someone interested in cities, the Global South is where to be.

Beyond that, there were three main goals going into the trip. One is to expand my journalistic coverage, exploring how Global South cities inform Market Urbanism. This theory, which I've covered extensively as founder of *Market Urbanism Report*, applies free-market policy ideas to city issues. Rooted from the classical liberal tradition, Market Urbanism calls for private-sector actions that create organic growth and voluntary exchange within cities, not ones enforced by government bureaucracy. I want to see how this high-level theory does (or does not) work in developing countries.

A second goal of my trip is to find investment opportunities, namely in a genre of privatized development that's come to be called "startup cities." These are common across the Global South, and I describe them below.

A third goal is to put on my consulting hat and discern which Global South urbanism lessons should be adopted by U.S. cities. That's the point of this essay.

The Pacific Research Institute recently launched the Free Cities Center to promote urban reform in the western United States, and invited me to contribute a piece on California.

The timing is apropos, because I just finished the Latin American portion of my trip (2023 will be Africa and Asia), which is the Global South region that California most resembles. I'll explain some urban policy concepts Latin America does well, and what the Golden State can learn from it.

California has a big Latino population whose culture goes largely untapped at the political level. Hispanics make up the largest ethnic group in California, with 40.2% of Californians identifying as such.[3] They lag in representation, making up 32.5% of the state Legislature.[4] More crucially, their ideas aren't reflected in the physical and cultural realm of how big California cities are planned. This means the state misses out on one benefit that usually comes from liberal immigration: new ideas.

Instead, cities like San Francisco, San Diego and Los Angeles are planning relics, functioning on the top-down motifs of post-World War II America.

The results are often ugly. California suffers from a government-imposed affordable home crisis while Latin America uses emergent urban forms to house its vast low-income population. Californian cities are wracked with congestion, auto-dependence and malfunctioning mass transit; Latin American cities have diverse, flexible, largely market-driven transport networks. California, while theoretically part of a nation with strong economic freedom and property rights, is itself an overtaxed and overregulated basket case. Latin America, while still suffering through socialism within various federal governments, enjoys a somewhat anarcho-capitalist sense of freedom at street level.

Thus, there is a gap in perception vs. reality between quality-of-life in "First World" California and "Third World" Latin America. While California remains a place many Latin Americans themselves gravitate to, it's far from perfect, and there are best practices it could adopt from its new incoming residents.

Below is a compilation of ones I discovered on my trip.

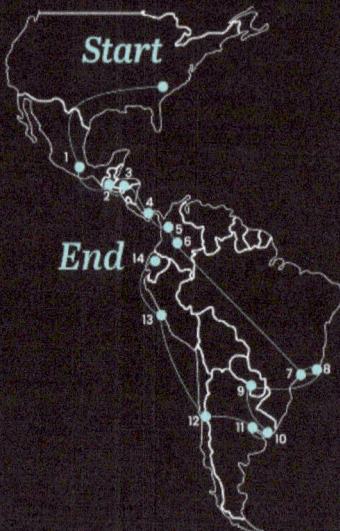

Beyer's Latin America Trip
July-December, 2022

1. Mexico City, Mexico
2. Guatemala City, Guatemala
3. Tegucigalpa, Honduras
4. Panama City, Panama
5. Medellin, Colombia
6. Bogota, Colombia
7. Sao Paulo, Brazil
8. Rio de Janeiro, Brazil
9. Asuncion, Paraguay
10. Montevideo, Uruguay
11. Buenos Aires, Argentina
12. Santiago, Chile
13. Lima, Peru
14. Quito, Ecuador

Start

End

Market
Urbanism
Report

Part 1: Housing

California's housing crisis is infamous, and has accelerated in recent years. The median single-family home price, as of April 2023, is over $800,000.[5] It's even worse in big cities like San Francisco and Los Angeles, where home prices average in the seven figures.

The high costs are driving people out. After the last census, California lost a congressional seat for the first time in its 171-year history.[6] California's population is growing more slowly than the rest of the nation. As the census showed in the last decade, the national population grew 7.4% while California's population grew 5.9%, from 37.3 million to 39.5 million residents. In the two years since those figures, California's population actually dropped by half a million people.[7]

A survey from the Public Policy Institute of California found that 70% of adults in California think housing affordability is a problem there. 34% of respondents say they would move from the state.[8]

Most Californians that flee head to nearby states with lower taxes and cheaper housing, such as Nevada, Idaho and Texas.[9]

California's population loss is a problem: when people leave, they take their tax dollars with them. This is problematic in a state that had a $32.5 billion budget deficit and over $500 billion[10] in state and local debt.

Even as people flee, housing prices remain high. It's not a problem of greedy landlords or overpopulation, but laws that make housing expensive and difficult to produce.

Latin America, a region full of people who make a fraction of California's median income, doesn't seem to have nearly the same level of housing insecurity. While it's hard to find apples-to-apples statistical comparisons, Latin American cities don't have nearly the visible homelessness found in Skid Row, the Tenderloin or other tent cities across urban California.

People also do not leave Latin American cities en masse – quite the opposite. The urban share of the population has grown region-wide through the decades, and many of those who migrate are destitute rural peasants who nonetheless find their place in big cities.[11]

Just consider: since 2010, Mexico City's metro population has grown by 9.7%;[12] Quito's by 18.4%;[13] and Sao Paulo's by 13.1%.[14] Other Latin American cities are similar and put California's paltry growth into perspective.

The reason Latin American cities can grow as such is that they function like amorphous organisms, handling population waves through ever-changing land use. California cities, by contrast, seem trapped in amber.

The difference lies in regulatory climate.

Zoning

Zoning is a regulation that governs land use and development. Such laws determine what can or can't be built in certain areas, deeming them residential, commercial, industrial, agricultural or other uses. Zoning laws also include building and development standards, such as building height, floor area ratio, lot setbacks, density levels and other physical aspects.

Many separate regulations complement zoning. Urban growth boundaries[15] lock off large portions of suburban land,[16] minimum parking requirements[17] force buildings to be surrounded by parking lots and environmental laws,[18] historic preservation districts[19] and other regulations[20] exert their control on the city-building process.

Cities in Europe and the United States are swallowed in such regulations. Note the general plan in any American municipality and one finds a simplistic document putting broad designations over large portions of land. Developer surveys conducted by the National Association of Homebuilders find that this regulatory soup adds 40% to the cost of multi-family housing.[21]

California is even worse than the rest of America. Nearly two-thirds of homes are single family residences, thanks to zoning laws that were only recently amended.[22] The under-utilization of land is particularly costly in big cities; for example, 38% of San Francisco's land is zoned single-family,[23] while that can be said of 77% of land[24] in greater Los Angeles.

In 2021, Gov. Gavin Newsom signed two laws to encourage denser development. The first, Senate Bill 9, allows homeowners with single-family lots to divide their lots in two and build more homes on them.[25] The other law, Senate Bill 10, allows cities to more easily up-zone areas near public transit, authorizing construction of up to 10 units on a single parcel.[26]

While such laws are a welcome change, they're mild and have not produced much new housing. California is 49th out of

50 states in per capita housing units.[27] The Wharton Index regularly ranks California metros as among the nation's most regulated for land use.[28]

Latin American cities operate on a totally different framework. While in theory not unregulated, it can seem that way, with much construction going where it's technically not supposed to.

One of my opening weekend stops on this trip was Monterrey, Mexico. A neighborhood there gave me insight into the spontaneous urbanism I would see region-wide.

Independencia, south of downtown, is considered dangerous, but didn't seem bad while I was walking through – and had fascinating land use. Seemingly devoid of zoning, the residential area had every last use mixed in: auto shops, small factories, salons, grocery marts, etc. Some businesses were literally run from people's homes, such as a guy selling hot dogs from his driveway. The neighborhood, despite being low-rise, was hyper-dense, with no vacant lots.

In Monterrey, a home and car repair shop sit side-by-side.

This neighborhood became a precursor for what I would find in middle- and upper-class Latin American ones, too. Fast-growing cities like Panama City, Medellín, São Paulo, Santiago and even Miami (the only true Latin American city in the United States) are all seeing massive amounts of high-rise construction, with single-family areas getting demolished and built anew.

While this verticality usually concentrates in specific zones, it spreads to others that one would not expect. I found in wealthy, low-rise gardenesque neighborhoods – such as Medellín's Laureles area – that developers were tearing down single-family homes to build five-to-10 story towers. This would be a non-starter in similar U.S. neighborhoods, squelched by restrictive zoning and historic preservation laws.

In Medellín's Poblado neighborhood, new skyscrapers rise all over.

Further downhill in Medellín's low-rise Laureles area, single-family homes get redeveloped into mid-rise towers.

This is partly because governments have no choice but to liberalize, given the demand pressures caused by the aforementioned rural migration. Some critics bemoan[29] this alleged overdevelopment, and there are in fact some zoning[30] laws that exist in such areas. But the laws are often flouted – a product of ignoring or bribing[31] one's way out of them.

It is within the Latin American context that California's state housing bills look mild, even ridiculous. While California's political class celebrates backyard cottages, Latin America's top cities are totally changing their skylines and overhauling core neighborhoods to handle the intense demand.

Favelas

But Latin America's truly unzoned order is found within informal settlements. These exist throughout the region (and the Global South) and have different names by country, including *barrios populares* in Ecuador, *pueblos jovenes* in Peru, and *favelas* in Brazil. For brevity's sake, I'll use that well-known latter term as a catchall for this development style.

Favela is the Portuguese word for "shantytown." Favelas are technically illegal, but they provide a significant amount of housing for those who otherwise cannot afford more standardized versions. They're typically occupied by rural migrants who flock into cities but cannot find housing, so they build these settlements in unorthodox places.

Brazil's favelas, for example, are typically built illegally on hills overlooking the city. There is extremely little space between homes, with narrow alleyways constructed based on cooperation between landowners. New structures are built in, up and around existing ones, via gradual construction.

Housing within favelas is low quality. They're built with whatever is available, like wood scraps, cardboard, metal sheets or plastic tarps. They lack infrastructure like plumbing and electricity. Sanitation is also an issue, due to lack of clean water and waste disposal systems.

Favelas aren't all bad, though, and to understand why, one need only compare them to the situation in California. Favelas provide deeply affordable housing for those at the bottom of the social hierarchy.[32] In various interviews, I found that units can rent for as low as a few dollars per month, and sell for a few thousand. Therefore, favelas function as a cure to homelessness, since most anyone can come up with those small rental payments.

The Vidigal favela in Rio de Janeiro

The San Antonio favela in Asuncion.

In California, homelessness continues to rise even while declining nationally.[33] There are many reasons, including the state's mental health and drug issues. But it's mostly because the rent is too damn high.

California tried addressing this problem by simply giving people houses, which is known as the "Housing First" model. Beginning in the George W. Bush administration,[34] the federal government encouraged cities to move away from transitional housing,[35] which stresses a "sobriety first" approach. Because many homeless people didn't want to sober up as a condition for shelter, the transitional model left them on the street.

By contrast, Housing First offers shelter as a baseline provision while using counseling to fix other problems that cause someone to be homeless. It has become accepted wisdom in the social services industry.

It's also been extremely expensive. San Francisco will spend $636 million on homelessness in 2023, and says it needs another $1.4 billion over three years to tackle the problem.[36] San Francisco says it needs 3,810 units of permanent housing and 2,250 shelter beds, in addition to social services. What's the reason for the high cost? A shelter bed in San Francisco costs $70,000[37] to build, while an "affordable" two-bedroom apartment costs $750,000.[38]

An audit found that one unit of housing for the homeless in Los Angeles costs as much as $837,000 to build.[39] Los Angeles City Controller Ron Galperin, who conducted the audit, blamed "bureaucracy," complaining that it takes years to finance units while the city is slow to approve them. Galperin called for the need "to clear away a lot of the debris of the many rules and impediments that government itself has put in place."[40]

Since it's so expensive for cities to provide permanent supportive homeless housing, the solution is not scalable and most homeless people end up in tents in the street.

In this sense, California cities veer between two extremes: the highly-standardized "Housing First" units, and the majority of homeless who don't win the lottery for them, and end up living in cars, RVs or tent encampments that ultimately get swept.

The California city closest to providing something in-between is San Jose. It used to spend $850,000 per unit[41] to build homes for the homeless, but has pivoted to "quick-build" apartments, which are pre-built modular units (like tiny homes).[42] They cost only $85,000 per unit and can be built in months instead of years.[43]

These apartments, made out of cheap materials, are probably the closest thing governments in California will get to endorsing favelas.

But there are other major differences besides the architecture: favelas are not only less standardized (and thus less expensive) but fall outside the framework of government planning altogether. They're effectively squatter settlements that result from illegal "invasions" of public land and thrive through self-governance.

In Part 3, I detail more about how such governance works, but the main takeaway here is that favelas affordably house the masses. Migrants settle on well-located urban land and build for themselves barebones accommodations. In California, these same people are homeless, and confined by law enforcement to live within dangerous open-air drug markets.

Labor Rules

A third factor that makes housing cheap in Latin America and expensive in California does not apply to land use, but construction: labor costs.

California has labor rules which add bloat to major housing projects (including some of the "Housing First" ones). When the state attempted to pass a law changing commercial zoning for vacant retail complexes, unions successfully blocked a key bill because it did not require union labor[44] (though a later compromise was achieved[45]).

Unions also campaign to expand project labor agreements to a growing number of construction projects.[46] PLAs, which govern the terms of construction, are commonplace in the state and are intended in part to bring stability to labor relations.[47] But according to RAND Corporation research, they increase project costs by as much as 15%. The study claimed that absent this arrangement, one Los Angeles affordable housing project would have cost $43,000 less per unit and 800 more units could have been included.[48]

In Latin America, labor laws are, like zoning laws, difficult to find online. That is because they mostly don't exist, though there are some international agreements and patchwork measures in place.[49] Compounding this lack of formal labor regulation is that, while public projects in California are subject to prevailing wage laws,[50] the market-based wages within Latin America are not very high (though some countries, including Brazil, do have minimum wage laws).

This means that public and private construction projects can hire hordes of workers. It's not uncommon to walk on job sites, such as a high-rise condo project I visited in the Honduran city Prospera, and see dozens or even hundreds of workers. This causes projects to finish quickly and at a much lower cost for the consumer.

Part 2: Transportation

Californians – and Americans generally – are hardwired to believe certain truisms about transportation, based on what we're used to.

We think that transport infrastructure and services must be government-run, and that those accommodations must necessarily be awful – marred by congestion, mismanagement, potholes and long dwell times.

These notions get challenged once Americans travel through Global South cities. There, people have managed to build private and public systems that are ubiquitous, affordable and high-quality – particularly in Latin America.

Private Transportation

Just as Mexico, my first stop, set the tone for how to view Latin American land use, so too did it help me understand the region's transportation philosophy.

I started in Mexico City, which is the largest city in North America but has a far different transit network than rivals like New York City and Toronto.

Sure, Mexico City still has a robust public transit system like those cities. Its vast metro rail[51] and bus rapid transit[52] network carries millions of passengers daily. But the city is so massive that public transportation doesn't cover the whole city. This means an even more impressive system of private buses – called "peseros" – has arisen to serve residents.[53]

Peseros are typically green and white, and seat around one or two dozen passengers. They are "flex route," following the whims of given drivers who thrive on local knowledge rather than set paths and schedules. Doors stay open so passengers can hop on or off anytime, and drivers stop whenever people flag them down, meaning the stops aren't limited either. Peseros were first seen in the 1970s, when they got their name for charging 1 peso. Even today they only charge 5 pesos (or USD $0.29) making them competitive with public transit and affordable to the working class.

As I found while riding one, the buses are modest. I handed the money directly to the driver, since there was no payment machine, and sat in the back of the vintage Mercedes vehicle. It soon filled up and became standing room only, as these buses often do. During the 15-minute ride, two teens came on to sell candy, followed by a young pair who performed a live Spanish rap duet.

So, the pesero experience is not remotely formal. But that doesn't mean it's a rinky-dink operation. Mexico City's pesero network is one of the world's largest bus systems. According to a Fast Company article, the system "accounts for 60% of all transit in the city, with about 14 million daily riders on 29,000 buses that run more than 1,500 routes."[54] The system is organic and largely unregulated; a given entrepreneur buys a bus, tacks on a sign, and hires a driver, who can then use public bus infrastructure and right-of-ways. However, peseros are declining in number as the city government cracks down, viewing them as a source of pollution and aggressive driving.

A tuktuk taxi serving Chorrillos, a favela in Lima.

This private transit provision model exists in every Latin American city. Because the services respond to market demand, they are very diverse. Along with jitney buses of varying size, I saw taxi services via motorbike, rickshaw and tuktuks.

These services are ubiquitous, efficiently routed and cheap, as competition drives fares down into the $0.10-$1 range, even without government subsidy.

The U.S. could have all this too, namely in California cities with the built-in advantage of relatively high population density. But the government prevents it.

Jitneys were once common across San Francisco, operated and patronized by the city's Latin American immigrants. The city disliked the competition to its public transit service, and in the early 1970s made jitney companies raise their fares to prevent undercutting MUNI. In 1978, the city stopped issuing permits altogether, causing gradual industry decline.[55]

Some 2011 reorganization in SFMTA created a brief period of deregulation, and like clockwork new jitneys surfaced, such as Chariot and Leap, two "Jitney 2.0" companies that emerged from Silicon Valley. But SFMTA was soon back harassing them, writing regulations that let the agency micromanage where they could stop, stating in the bylaws that "routes must complement, rather than compete with, Muni."[56] SFMTA also authorized permit fees, limits on vehicle length and mandates that companies share data with the city.

Within a few years, Leap[57] and Chariot[58] had both gone out of business.

San Francisco has made similar crackdowns on rideshare, bikeshare and scootershare companies (while ironically viewing itself as a hub for experimental technology). This means a nascent and potentially vast micro-mobility industry was not allowed to scale in a city where it was enjoying clear market proof.

It's too bad, because San Francisco riders could use an alternative. Since the pandemic, public transit ridership has plummeted. The SFMTA reports that ridership is two-thirds of what it was pre-pandemic, leaving the agency short on cash.[59] They say they will need to cut service unless they receive a $5.1 billion subsidy from the state (which recently was agreed to by the governor and legislators).[60]

The Latin America example suggests that San Francisco shouldn't need these subsidies, or possibly public transit service at all. Just as market actors provide food, housing and everything else, even in poor regions, they will provide transit within dense cities where people must get around.

Public transit

That said, Latin America still has very good public transit. The presence of private transit there hasn't "cannibalized" from the government option – a common critique among transit activists. Instead, both frameworks bolster each other.

Latinos are an urban populace, which explains the need for such systems. Elaborating on that rural-to-urban-migration theme, the World Economic Forum predicts that by 2050, 90% of Latinos will live in cities.[61] Already, transit systems comprise 68% of all passenger travel in Latin America.[62] The public ones account for 14% of travel in Mexico City and Lima, and 12% in Buenos Aires and Rio de Janeiro.[63]

Despite Latin American countries having a fraction of U.S. per-capita income, they run objectively better systems than most any U.S. city. While not "slick" like Asian transit systems, they are quite functional.

Bus Rapid Transit (BRT) began in 1974 in Curitiba, Brazil.[64] Having visited, I found its system approximates light rail. Loading platforms are separated from the street and equal to bus height (features also seen in Mexico City, Guatemala City and Bogota), allowing for step-free boarding. These loading-platforms-cum-stations are enclosed; have off-bus fare payment; and most crucially are connected to dedicated lanes. Curitiba was also an early pioneer in accepting electronic payment (2002) and real-time bus tracking.[65] In the United States, these features rolled out only recently.

As The Transportation Research Board found, "with good planning and organization busways can carry high volumes of passengers at reasonable commercial speeds – equivalent to those of [light rail] or tram technology under the same operating environment."[66] Indeed, Curitiba's system ridership is high – in 2007, a stunning 70% of commuters used the system, and ridership was 5 million, with cheap fares.[67]

The BRT system in Curitiba.

Bogota's TransMilenio is another high-ridership network. Launched in 1999, the system is now "the largest BRT in the world," and through its existence road fatalities have dropped 92% along its corridors. Like in Curitiba, development occurred rapidly – in its first year of operation, TransMilenio rolled out about 25 miles of dedicated bus lanes.[68]

Other cities – including Buenos Aires, Santiago and Panama City – have well-developed subway systems. And Latin American transit agencies have even begun rolling out metro-

The Panama Metro, at once basic yet modern and functional.

cable lines to improve mobility in their many hillside favelas.[69] The most famous example, which I detail further down, are the lines in Medellín connecting the Comuna 13 slum with the city proper. The system only cost $71 million and carries 20,000 passengers daily.

Contrast this with California, where comparably simple bus lane projects take years. San Francisco built its first BRT line on Van Ness Avenue. It's two miles long and has nine stops. The bus lane took 27 years and cost $300 million.[70] The project took so long because of California's complex and burdensome rules. After the project was funded by Proposition K in 2003,[71] it underwent a Feasibility Study in 2006.[72] Then in 2011, the project went through environmental review.

The project was finally approved by the San Francisco Board of Supervisors in 2013.

The project officially broke ground in 2016, but suffered from construction delays. The water and sewer lines had to be replaced, which was the main reason for the delay. The city underwent litigation with a contractor and had to offer compensation to businesses on Van Ness that were impacted by the long construction time. Finally, the BRT opened in 2022.[73]

Of course, this is one small project. The bigger they get, the more riddled they become by waste and delay, with California's high-speed rail serving as perhaps the ultimate example of this in America.[74]

Thing is, there is demand in California for such public transit projects (just as there is for private transit). The Van Ness BRT, despite its problematic rollout, has been a success. Ridership increased by 60%[75] and riders saved 35%[76] in travel times. San Francisco has implemented another BRT route on Geary Street.[77]

The problem is that San Francisco and other U.S. cities don't complete these projects fast enough to make a dent. Latin America does for various reasons. Its autocratic legacy, in contrast with California's hyper-localist democracies, means snap decisions can be made about public right-of-way. While visiting Curitiba, a former staffer of the late mayor Jaime Lerner (the BRT mastermind) recalled how he would execute his public works in the middle of the night, without informing interested parties. They would wake up the next day for a surprise. This would never fly in the United States – and that's probably good.

But Latin America also builds lots of cost-effective transit for the same reason it builds lots of cheap housing. There are fewer environmental laws, labor rights, NIMBY rent-seekers, and other project-stopping legalities than in the United States. This means Latin America gets more done with less.

Toll Roads

Another Latin American transport innovation has been its tolling of roads.

One success story occurred in Honduras. It's a poor country and most roads are in terrible shape; I had to pay large repair costs after driving on Roatan Island (the last time during this trip I dared rent a car). But the nation's main highway, the mountain-splitting CA5, functions better than most U.S. interstates.

Honduras entered a public-private partnership with the road management firm COVI to operate it.[78] This saved taxpayer money, since the company was the one investing funds into the project, and has an incentive to cut costs and give better customer service. The CA5 privatization has also saved Hondurans money and time – it costs a few dollars to drive the 3.5 hours from Tegucigalpa to San Pedro Sula. In Global South countries I've visited that don't have these modernized interstates, such a trip can take 10 hours and do tremendous damage to one's car.

Honduras' CA5

Another country that uses privatized roads is Brazil. It has suffered from public resource shortages, which has led to deterioration of road quality.[79] To escape the crisis, they began working with private companies in 1995 through concessions, and then formally created a law to establish public-private partnerships in 2005. Brazil now has about 70 toll facilities. Most are operated by private companies.[80]

California has experimented with road privatization. San Diego had a PPP, the first in California, called the South Bay Expressway. It was meant to connect San Diego with its fast-growing suburbs. Caltrans, the department that operates roads in California, worked with a private concessionaire, SBX. The company agreed to finance and construct the roadway, then transfer the title back to Caltrans after construction was completed.[81] Then, Caltrans gave operational rights to SBX to collect tolls on the road.

Construction began in 2003 and was completed in 2007. Unfortunately, the road opened at the height of the subprime mortgage crisis. Suburban areas of San Diego were hit hard and toll revenues were far lower than expected; in 2010, SBX went bankrupt.[82]

While people consider the project a failure, privatization supporters argue that these deals, however bad for the operator, still take liabilities off taxpayers. Baruch Feigenbaum, a transport analyst for Reason, writes that the San Diego deal protected taxpayers and delivered results faster than a government-facilitated program would have, taking the long-delayed proposal from an idea debated by local governments to implementation.[83] Then, of course, there are the dozens of toll roads across America that don't fail, either profiting as stand-alone private entities or providing revenue streams for state governments. This tends to happen in states, such as Florida[84] and Texas,[85] that are better known than California for getting things done. And it seems to be working in Latin America.

Motorbikes

I wrote above that motorbikes are sometimes used in Latin America for transit. It's not uncommon to wave them down and hop on for a ride, which seldom costs more than a few bucks.

But motorbikes' main use in Latin America is to deliver food and goods – and what a use it has become. There's now a private sector war to dominate regional delivery, and the battles play out differently in each country. Large foreign firms like Uber (U.S.), Glovo (Spain) and Didi (China)[86] compete with homegrown ones like Rappi (Colombia), PedidosYa (Uruguay) and iFood (Brazil).[87] This being the Global South, there are also many sole proprietors who carve their small slice from the market, visiting social media to read people's delivery requests and arrange with them prices and delivery times.

This has caused Latin American streets to become absolutely flooded with motorbike delivery guys, complementing those who use the mode for commuting. Household motorbike and moped ownership in many Latin American countries is around 20-30%,[88] and anecdotally, that seems to be the percentage of trips they account for.

No U.S. city has anywhere close to this saturation – not even in California, once famous for its motorcycle culture.

It should be stressed that, unlike other topics I've covered, this one is less about policy than culture. Latin America has many

SCOTT BEYER

people using these bikes because they enjoy them, and it's all they can afford. But cities there have facilitated the culture through permissive hands-off governance.

Latin American motorbikers are granted extreme liberties in carving out right-of-way. In Brazil, the practice of lane-splitting (driving between both cars on a two-lane interstate) is so common that it produces invisible 'third lanes' that drivers respect. Elsewhere, I found large clusters of motorbikes parked along curbsides or even on sidewalks, as deliverymen loiter there between orders.

It's impossible to say whether U.S. cities would be this permissive if faced with motorbiking demand at this scale. But the answer is likely "no."

A gaggle of PedidosYa deliverymen in Panama City.

Aside from delivery, motorbikes are crucial for commuting in Latin America, including in this village outside Cartagena.

U.S. cities, including in California, have generally been hostile to micro-mobility vehicles, shared services or anything else that threatens the large vehicle hierarchy.[89] Revel mopedshare launched three years ago in San Francisco,[90] and it waits to be seen whether that city is more welcoming than New York has been.[91]

It's too bad, because mass motorbike adoption in Latin America has done much to make crowded road networks more efficient. Motorbikes consume less space, apply less weight on road surfaces and make deliveries cheaper for consumers.

Part 3:
Planning and Administration

Despite Latin America's great recent economic gains, it's still a place known for corrupt and unstable governments. Many countries swing between right-wing authoritarianism and left-wing socialism, depending on who is in charge at the moment.

Still, there are things within Latin America planning and administration that are uniquely better than the United States. I'll stick to three examples from the built landscape, since larger macro-economic and macro-political issues, such as monetary policy, would be a rabbit hole.

Barrios tropicales

Walking through parts of Medellín feels like navigating a jungle. Sure, it's a big developing world city with lots of concrete, but in famed neighborhoods like Laureles and Poblado, one is treated to an array of verdant green fauna along sidewalks, balconies and parks. It's a common aesthetic within wealthy neighborhoods of other big Latin American cities, enough that I coined a term for them: *barrios tropicales*, or tropical neighborhoods.

Laureles, Medellín

Laureles, on Medellín's west side, fits the bill. The neighborhood began in the 1930s with a plan from urbanist Pedro Nel Gomez, who wanted it built on a circular and transversal grid inspired by Paris.[92] It was supposed to have meadows, fountains and gardens, envisioned as a pastoral escape from the gritty urban center for Colombia's working class (the original proposed name was "The Citadel of the Employee"). However, it has attracted wealthy residents[93] and was renamed Laureles, after the laurel trees in the area, and is now one of Medellín's most exclusive areas.

Like other Latin American barrios tropicales, ones in Medellín became tropical due to a mix of public and private investment.

In Laureles, many of the verdant parks, boulevards and streets date back to that original plan. But some come more recently, due to a city initiative to fight the urban heat island effect.

Medellín has created 30 "green corridors" maintained by hundreds of gardeners along 18 streets and 12 bodies of water.[94] The program installed plants including native trees, tropical plants, bamboo and palms, and is maintained by hundreds of gardeners.[95] The corridors soak up pollution, create shade and provide havens for wildlife.

But another component of barrios tropicales comes from the private sector. Commercial storefronts and residential buildings, looking to compete for upscale clients in these areas, bolster their look with hanging balcony gardens, planter boxes and ivy-covered walls. There is even a Spanish phrase for the "mini-forests" that building owners plant in their front yards as a status symbol.

A linear park in Laureles, Medellín.

While Medellín had the most barrios tropicales of any Latin American city I visited, others had their own unique features. In Rio de Janeiro, the Leblon neighborhood placed this aesthetic along the beach, helping explain why it has among LatAm's highest real estate values.[96] Mexico City's Condesa mixes the aesthetic with its historic art deco buildings. Some barrios tropicales, such as Punta Carretas in Montevideo, are not technically in tropical climates, but still achieve the look by planting trees sooner associated with the Northern Hemisphere.

No U.S. neighborhood – not even in California – is a barrio tropical based on the four criteria listed above. But there's a nationwide movement towards greener cities, often fueled by studies showing the environmental and economic benefits of street trees. The Inflation Reduction Act gave $1.5 billion to the U.S. Forest Service's Urban and Community Forestry Program so cities can plant trees.[97]

Condesa in Mexico City.

California also gives grants to cities through its Urban Greening Program. The program funds the expansion of community spaces and parks, tree planting and green infrastructure in streets and alleys.[98]

One city that used the grant to create a downtown similar to a barrio tropical is Coachella,[99] which received $3.19 million in 2018.[100] As part of the The Grapefruit Boulevard Urban Greening and Connectivity Project, they planted 288 trees and plants. The plants provide aesthetic value, and also help moderate temperatures, clean the air and provide shade for pedestrians.

Another city in California that is very green is Sacramento, nicknamed the "City of Trees." Treepedia, a project run by MIT, measured tree coverage in cities and found that Sacramento is America's greenest city, with 23.6% tree coverage.[101]

Sacramento wasn't originally like that. When Gold Rush settlers arrived in Sacramento, it was mostly covered in grasses. They planted trees for shade to deal with the hot summers. First, they introduced eucalyptus trees from Australia. Later they brought in elm trees, which are common on the East Coast, then palms and fruit trees.[102] Both private organizations and government participated in the planting, which increased civic pride.

As of November 2022, California allocated $156.5 million for urban greening projects.[103] But no matter the level of government funds spent, the main barriers to a U.S. barrio tropical are cultural. Many private property owners nowadays don't see the value-add of urban forestry, whether it's them or the public that is footing maintenance costs.

And many U.S. city neighborhoods frankly aren't "urban" enough to fit the barrio tropical look. But some of the ones in San Diego and Los Angeles (a concrete jungle if there is one) would be leading candidates. They already have the urban "bones," along with the climates and tropical native plant life. It's just a matter of public and private actors recognizing this and unifying to green up their surroundings. If they need proof that this pays for itself through higher land values, they can look to Latin America's barrios tropicales, many of which have become international destinations.

Favelas

I described above the role that favelas play in providing deeply affordable housing. But it's worth looking into their governing structure itself, which might appeal to free-market urbanists.

Favela governance has long been mysterious to outsiders, developing localized systems that are understood only by those living within. Brazilian ones began in the late 19th century when soldiers settled in the hills of Rio de Janeiro.[104] They proliferated from the 1940s to 1970s, when rural Brazilians moved from the countryside to cities. Other such neighborhoods came later depending on the country. While overlooking the vast urban sprawl of Quito from a nearby mountain, my guide explained that much of it had been built illegally in the last two decades, a process he witnessed firsthand through the years while hiking.

The illegal nature of favelas go hand-in-hand with lack of general rule of law. Favelas have consistently struggled with high crime and gang control. They generally don't have well-established property rights – in fact, the lack of property demarcation fuels violence. Hernando de Soto writes in *The Mystery of Capital* that bribery is a huge tax in these areas, at the hands either of local mafias or government officials.[105]

Much of the Quito development visible here occurred the last couple decades, and illegally.

But there's another angle, which de Soto covers, that makes them seem freer than many "legal" neighborhoods. This too has to do with the absence of government.

Private actors rise up to provide buses, schools, policing, trash collection and more. Their systems are often market-driven and self-regulating. Other times, though, the services become cartelized, aping a problem found in government provision.

But more compelling to libertarians is the way in which these favelas *aren't* regulated. Let's start with the land use itself, which features typologies that would never be allowed (especially given where they are built) under normal zoning. Favelas have no apparent setbacks, use designations or design controls, much less the parking minimums that outlaw so many building types in the United States. Construction is incremental, in that households start with small structures and build around and above them as their needs change (creating the "stacking" aesthetic in these areas).

But this liberalization extends to businesses. Favelas are low-barrier-to-entry neighborhoods where any sole proprietor can set up shop. So these areas become like linear Walmarts, with every last thing getting sold from stores, carts, tents and even buckets that people carry on their heads.

A street market within a Santiago favela.

This is not to romanticize the conditions in favelas – they are places with high crime, raw sewage, dangerous electrical hookups and other problems. This is largely due to the fact that they don't enjoy the government subsidies other neighborhoods do, nor are they serving a wealthy clientele.

But to paraphrase the great Thomas Sowell, things should be judged only by how they compare to the alternatives. It's worth judging the lifestyle of favela residents with extremely low-income people in California. The state has 115,000 homeless people, many of whom live in truly substandard conditions on the street.[106] There is no ability for them to organize and build their own self-autonomous communities, because public land, unlike in Latin America, is locked off from squatters.

This caused one United Nations official to remark that conditions for California's extremely poor are worse than in the Third World, because they have no ability to access even the basic provisions (such as a rooftop) found in shantytowns.[107]

But the lessons from favelas go beyond the homeless. America has increasingly become crimped by occupational licensure, which is now needed for 30% of jobs.[108] There is something refreshing about communities where people with no education and credentials can operate unlicensed wherever consumers demand it.

Gradually, Latin American cities are improving their favelas through infrastructure investment. Once favelas build enough critical mass to become political blocs, officials start extending services there. Private investment soon joins and these neighborhoods gentrify, with shacks getting demolished to build standard structures, representing the next iteration in these emergent urban neighborhoods.

That shouldn't be surprising, given that favelas often possess lots of character: walkable, amenity-rich, close to jobs. They're perhaps the ultimate Jane Jacobs neighborhoods.

One of the oldest favelas in Argentina is Villa 31, near one of Buenos Aires' wealthiest areas. Most of its 40,000 residents lack running water, sewage service and electricity. The government is investing $320 million to improve homes, build a bank, schools and restaurants.[109] Given the location and design of Villa 31, I think it's just a matter of time before its real estate becomes valuable.

Villa 31 in Buenos Aires.

The Vidigal neighborhood in Rio de Janeiro is one of the many that the city "pacified," using aggressive police tactics to weed out gangs. While not totally safe, it has lured in tourists who drink at hilltop bars and overlook the city.

Medellín's Comuna 13 is Latin America's ultimate example of slum revitalization. High up on a steep hill and without a connective street network, it was once among the world's most dangerous places.

In 2004, the government began building gondolas – now called the Metrocable – to connect Comuna 13 to the city. In 2011, they built a giant, 384-meter covered outdoor escalator to make commuting up and down the mountain easier.[110]

Comuna 13 in Medellin.

Now, Comuna 13 is one of Latin America's leading tourist spots, as neighborhood residents responded to these investments by starting businesses and painting murals.

California cities want to "pacify" their slums. Los Angeles' Skid Row received $47.5 million in state funding in 2022. The city will use the money to build 2.4 miles of bicycle infra-structure, plant 500 trees and install 540 pedestrian lights. It will also widen sidewalks and create new bicycle connections. Additionally, the city plans to build a public plaza.[111] San Francisco Mayor London Breed has made better safety in the Tenderloin an anchor of her campaign.[112]

But I'm skeptical, as California's governing model comes with a degree of "process" that doesn't exist at street level most anywhere in Latin America. The likelier outcome is that these cities spend lots of money and nothing gets fixed, when they could just as soon look at the "unplanning" of favelas to find cheaper, more effective solutions.

Part 4: Startup Cities

I've described in this essay lots of flaws within the California system – overregulation, protectionism, and other public choice problems that arise from over-reliance on government. Frankly these exist in Latin America too, beyond the narrow set of positive case studies I've described.

The key for people in both regions is to have an escape valve, an option for alternative governing models that compete with the old ones. That is where "startup cities" come in.

These are entrepreneurial ventures to build and manage cities. They are private sector efforts to develop urban environments, with the goal not only to profit, but to test living arrangements that are more innovative than what government-run cities now do.

There are three kinds of startup cities, according to Adrianople Group, a global consulting firm that specializes in this genre and documents their emergence.[113]

The first is more or less a conventionally-governed city "that attracts startups." San Jose and other cities within Silicon Valley are examples.

The second type is another standard government municipality that "acts like a startup," based on degree of entrepreneurial activity, drawing on rankings by the Innovation Cities Index. Dubai is one example.

But the third, and most interesting, category refers to cities which are themselves startups. These private cities are distinct from municipal governments, which run on democracy and through publicly-appointed administrators; instead they often leave decisions to a CEO and board of investors. Startup cities even differ from workaday private city governments, such as the homeowners' associations in the United States, as they look to build communities that are dense, urban and focused on cutting-edge business concepts.

Some startup cities still work with governments. Many enjoy "special economic zone," status that their host governments created to attract economic development and foreign investment. Usually people and businesses in SEZs receive incentives and tax benefits. The cities often have looser regulations so businesses can operate freely.

California has one community, Irvine, that is a startup city, in that it began as a private project before later incorporating and adopting a democratic system.[114] Other U.S. examples of privatized or semi-autonomous governance include Sandy Springs, Georgia,[115] Reston, Virginia, and Culdesac,[116] an experimental car-free community getting built outside Phoenix.

However, Latin America and the Global South generally is teeming with startup cities, enough that this has become a focus of my trip. My goal is to visit several dozen and rank them based on planning, investment quality and other metrics. I'm calling it

Prospera, a city based on Roatan Island

"The Startup Cities Tour," and results have been published on *Market Urbanist.*

One early leader in startup city creation is Honduras. It's perhaps the toughest place to live in Latin America, with the region's second-highest murder rate, its highest poverty rate and a history of corruption. I experienced some of this while visiting in August, staying primarily in the capital, Tegucigalpa, and witnessing firsthand the dangerous living standards, even hearing gunshots up the hill from my hotel.[117]

Some Honduran leaders wished to induce alternative "charter city" governance that let Hondurans escape this system without having to leave their homeland. A decade ago, they passed legislation authorizing development zones that would largely operate autonomously from Honduras' federal government. These

SCOTT BEYER

Zones for Economic Development and Employment (ZEDEs) could experiment with different models.

Most special economic zones only allow for industrial development. ZEDEs, though, allow for the creation of whole cities with more liberal trade and development policy.

Already two ZEDEs are being built – both of which I visited – although their status remains uncertain under Honduras' newly elected left-wing government.[118]

The best-known one is Prospera, a city based on Roatan Island. The company's building a private city based on common law principles. Along with extremely low taxes and regulations, it will become somewhat of a testing ground for policy best practices, with liberal zoning, private education, medical freedom and

Cayalá, in Guatemala City.

Bitcoin as a legal tender. Prospera also features a modernized financial center and an online citizenship platform.

Gabriel Ayau, a city co-founder, told me the goal is to foster a "Latin American Singapore" in Honduras – although they also want to build other Prosperas in different countries.

Michatoya Pacifico, still under construction.

A second Honduran startup city, Ciudad Morazán, wants to establish an industrial hub–but with housing. Morazán is based outside San Pedro Sula, a city with lots of SEZs and, partly as a result, that is dangerous. Job-seeking migrants move near the SEZ factories but, absent any housing, form illegal favelas that become gang-controlled.

The promise of Morazán is to house these workers secure-
ly, which again is made possible by the pro-housing details of
the ZEDE law. Already Morazán has completed some industrial
warehouses and is building cheap workforce rental housing.

But long-term, explained project manager Diego Zuniga
Aguilera, Morazán wants to become a whole big private city.
They're planning for 15,000 residents in under a square mile – a
high density level – and those residents can start their own businesses, schools and transit services. Morazán, which was founded
by pro-liberty investor Massimo Mazzone, has its own private
police force, a particularly salient need given Honduras' history
of police corruption.

But Honduras isn't the only Latin American country leading on startup cities. In Guatemala, I visited two that were interesting in their differences, showing the broad utilization of
the concept.

Within Guatemala City's limits the government allowed
the Cayalá development to be built up a hillside. While it doesn't
have special jurisdiction status, it clearly enjoyed a hands-off
approval process that would be near-impossible to imagine in
modern America.[119]

Cayalá is like a neo-traditional community that was stolen
from Europe and planted into Guatemala City, but in no way
mirrors its surroundings. It has fancy restaurants, civic plazas,
Mediterranean architecture and all parking is underground. Two
hours away, in a rural area close to the port, a different developer
is building Michatoya Pacifico.[120] It aims to be an industrial city
for poor rural dwellers, with its own toll road connecting to Guatemala City.[121]

In Florianopolis, Brazil, I visited Jurere Internacional.[122] Once a government municipality, the development firm Grupo Habitasul purchased part of the city to manage it privately. They refurbished the beachfront community by building pedestrian malls, beach clubs and an entertainment park – all measures that throw value back into their residential holdings. Meanwhile the government-run portion of Jurere still sits next to this private portion, invoking yet another Latin American governance framework that would be hard to imagine in the United States.

My biggest surprise was how adamant all these startup cities (even the industrial-focused ones) were in touting their safe, tree-lined, multi-modal streets, showing they recognized the economic benefits of the *barrio tropical* aesthetic.

One example is Porta Norte, in Panama City.[123] It plans to be denser and more modern than most places, but also more thoughtfully planned. CEO Henry Faarup told me the streets will be the lead selling point. Panamanians are tired of hot, dangerous streets. Porta Norte's will feature 50 tree species, with a different species on each block. They'll be allowed to grow out, creating "tree ceilings" to block the sun.

California doesn't have special economic zones or even many startup cities, but allowing them could quell unrest. Since people don't have the option to create their own cities, they go for more extreme solutions, like secession or dividing the state.

California's far-north region has long felt ignored by politicians in Sacramento. People there have proposed a new state called Jefferson that would also include southern Oregon.[124] The Jefferson movement gained strength in the years before World War II, and was revived in 2013 when various northern California counties, including Siskiyou, Modoc, Glenn, Yuba and Tehama voted to withdraw from California.[125]

Another proposal was made by venture capitalist Tim Draper to split the state into three states. He argued that California was too large and ungovernable and that three states would be more efficient. Amazingly, his plan received enough signatures to place a proposition on the November 2018 ballot.[126] However, the California state supreme court removed it when an environmental group complained.[127]

To that point: California is likely too captured by regulation to ever lead on startup cities. Donald Bren, owner and chairman of the Irvine Company, said himself that Irvine would never happen today, citing the state's environmental laws.

A group of venture capitalists has bought 50,000 acres of ranchland in Solano County, between the San Francisco Bay Area and the Sacramento region, with an eye toward building a brand new city. It's a fascinating proposal, but will face numerous local and state regulatory hurdles.

But the whole governing "vibe" of Latin America suggests it's the perfect place for startup cities. Just as hordes of migrants can invade public land and build favelas, large developers can assemble land and build their dream communities.

Faarup echoed other startup city developers I interviewed when he said about the Panama City government's approach to Porta Norte: "they pretty much just let us do what we wanted."

Conclusion

Latin America doesn't have perfect governance. The United States may have individual socialist politicians like Bernie Sanders and Alexandria Ocasio-Cortez, but socialism is more built into Latin America's political history and fabric. A recent "pink tide" saw leftist leaders get elected in Mexico, Chile, Peru and Brazil.[128]

Socialist leaders have been a disaster for Latin American economies. Ones like Argentina and Venezuela experienced hyperinflation, making it difficult for people to afford basic needs. Unstable economies scare away investors. Crime is also a major problem. In a list of the world's 50 most violent cities, 38 are in Latin America.[129]

This isn't a surprise to anyone. Over 2 million migrants, mostly from Latin America, tried to cross the southern border in 2022.[130] They say they're fleeing violence, persecution, lack of food and political instability. Many are simply looking for better economic opportunities.

California is still seen as a land of opportunity for many. Silicon Valley is still a global center of innovation. That, and its proximity to the Mexican border, is why Latino immigrants move there.

But six months of travel through Latin America gave too nuanced a view to say one region is point-blank "bad" and the other "good." For all its opportunities, California drowns in an administrative apparatus that threatens the state's future. Its real poverty rate, when accounting for living costs, is the nation's highest.[131] It has increasingly become a state where it's hard to achieve the basics of the American dream – homeownership, business formation and freedom of movement.

Meantime in Latin America, for all its high-level socialism, seems freer at street level – a place where it's easier to do all these things.

California shouldn't copy everything about Latin America. But officials might look into the best aspects of its urban policy.

Pieces of this essay were readapted from Scott Beyer's Independent Institute column.

Endnotes

1   Scott Beyer, "Scott Beyer's Market Urbanism World Trip," *Market Urbanism Report,* https://marketurbanismreport.com/scott-beyer-market-urbanism-world-trip

2   Avery Koop, "Ranked: The World's Fastest Growing Cities," *Visual Capitalist*, August 13, 2021, https://www.visualcapitalist.com/ranked-the-worlds-fastest-growing-cities/

3   "Quick Facts: California," United States Census Bureau, July 1, 2022, https://www.census.gov/quickfacts/fact/table/CA/PST045222

4   Matthew Miranda, "A record number of Latino lawmakers are heading to California's Capitol after midterm election," *The Sacramento Bee*, December 5, 2022, https://www.sacbee.com/news/politics-government/capitol-alert/article269226512.html

5   "April home sales and price report: Higher mortgage rates and low housing inventory restrain California home sales in April, C.A.R reports," California Association of Realtors, May 18, 2023, https://www.car.org/en/aboutus/mediacenter/newsreleases/2023-News-Releases/april2023sales

6   Ben Christopher, "California loses congressional seat for first time," *CalMatters*, April 26, 2021 (updated May 6, 2021), https://calmatters.org/politics/2021/04/california-congress-census/

7   Marc Cota-Robles and Grace Manthey, "California's population drops by more than half a million people in span of 2 years," *ABC 7 Eyewitness News (Los Angeles)*, February 16, 2023, https://abc7.com/are-people-leaving-california-where-should-i-move-to-housing-in-moving/12826300/

8   Mark Baldassare, Dean Bonner, Rachel Lawler, and Deja Thomas, "PPIC Statewide Survey: Californians and Their Government," Public Policy Institute of California, February 2023, https://www.ppic.org/publication/ppic-statewide-survey-californians-and-their-government-february-2023/

9   Soumya Karlamangla, "Texas? Idaho? Where Californians are Moving," *The New York Times,* September 2, 2021, https://www.nytimes.com/2021/09/02/us/where-californians-are-moving.html

10   "State and local government debt in California from fiscal year 1999 to 2021 with a forecast to 2027 (in billion U.S. dollars)," Statista Research Department, September 30, 2022, https://www.statista.com/statistics/305287/california-state-debt/

11   Glenn Hyman, "Rural and urban population growth in Latin America (absolute and proportional)," from Glenn Hyman, Sam Fujisaka, and Mariano Mejia, "Regional Literature Review on Ecosystem Services and Poverty Alleviation: The Desakota Assessment: Amazon and Andes," International Centre for Tropical Agriculture, accessed via Research Gate, https://www.researchgate.net/figure/Rural-and-urban-population-growth-in-Latin-America-between-1970-and-2000-Hyman-et-al_fig1_242574869

12   "Mexico City, Mexico Metro Area Population 1950-2023," *Macro-Trends*, https://www.macrotrends.net/cities/21853/mexico-city/population

13   "Quito, Ecuador Metro Area Population 1950-2023," *MacroTrends*, https://www.macrotrends.net/cities/20910/quito/population

14   "Sao Paulo, Brazil Metro Area Population 1950-2023," *MacroTrends*, https://www.macrotrends.net/cities/20287/sao-paulo/population

15   See "Urban Development Boundaries," Annual CALAFCO Conference, September 2015, p. 3, https://calafco.org/sites/default/files/resources/Urban_Grwoth_Boundaries_all_in_one.pdf, which states "California requires each county to have a Local Agency Formation Commission, which sets urban growth boundaries for each city and town in the county."

16   Scott Beyer, "The Folly of 'Growth Management' Policies," *Catalyst*, September 10, 2020, https://catalyst.independent.org/2020/09/10/growth-management-policies

17 Christian Britschgi, "California Takes on the High Cost of Mandated Parking," *Reason,* August 30, 2022, https://reason.com/2022/08/30/california-takes-on-the-high-cost-of-mandated-parking

18 Baruch Feigenbaum, "CEQA's Burdensome Regulation Abuses Power and Decreases Housing Availability," *Reason*, May 2, 2017, https://reason.org/commentary/ceqas-burdensome-regulation-abuses/

19 "The Art of Camouflaging NIMBYism," *UrbanizeLA*, November 11, 2015, https://la.urbanize.city/post/art-camouflaging-nimbyism. Also see, for example, the City of Santa Rosa's historic preservation review regulations ("Processing Review Procedures for Owners of Historic Properties," Cultural Heritage Board of the City of Santa Rosa, January 9, 2001, https://www.srcity.org/DocumentCenter/View/3259/Processing-Review-Procedures-for-Owners-of-Historic-Properties---PDF), which describes the "design review" process that alterations to historic-designated properties must undergo.

20 For instance, San Diego forbids construction of buildings taller than 30 feet along most of its coastline; see "Determination of Building Height in the Coastal Height Limitation Overlay Zone," City of San Diego Development services, August 2013, https://www.sandiego.gov/sites/default/files/legacy/development-services/pdf/industry/techbulletin/bldg-5-4.pdf

21 Paul Emrath and Caitlin Sugrue Walker, "Regulation: 40.6 Percent of the Cost of Multifamily Development," National Association of Homebuilders, 2022, 2022-nahb-nmhc-cost-of-regulations-report.pdf

22 John Healey and Matthew Ballinger, "What just happened with single-family zoning in California?," *Los Angeles Times*, September 17, 2021, https://www.latimes.com/homeless-housing/story/2021-09-17/what-just-happened-with-single-family-zoning-in-california

23 Sriharsha Devtriapalli, "This map shows the parts of SF zoned for single-family homes," *San Francisco Chronicle,* January 9, 2023, https://www.sfchronicle.com/sf/article/sf-map-single-family-homes-17699820.php

24 Stephen Menendian, Samir Gambhir, and Chih-Weh Hsu, "Single-Family Zoning in Greater Los Angeles," Othering & Belonging Institute, March 2, 2022, https://belonging.berkeley.edu/single-family-zoning-greater-los-angeles

25   "SB 9 (Atkins): The California H.O.M.E Act," California State Senate,
      https://focus.senate.ca.gov/sb9

26   "Senate Floor Analyses: SB-10: Planning and zoning: housing devel-
      opment: density (2021-2022)," August 25, 2021, accessed via California
      Legislative Information https://leginfo.legislature.ca.gov/faces/billA-
      nalysisClient.xhtml?bill_id=202120220SB10

27   Chris Nichols, "TRUE: California ranks 49th in per-capita housing
      supply," *PolitiFact*, March 21, 2018, https://www.politifact.com/fact-
      checks/2018/mar/21/gavin-newsom/true-california-ranks-49th-capi-
      ta-housing-supply/

28   Paul Emrath, "Updated Index Shows Regulation Most Restrictive
      on the Coasts," National Association of Home Builders, January 13,
      2020, https://eyeonhousing.org/2020/01/updated-index-shows-regula-
      tion-most-restrictive-on-the-coasts/

29   "Housing in Latin America," *The World of Teoalida*, https://www.teoali-
      da.com/world/latinamerica/

30   Amanda Briney, "Latin America City Structure Model," *ThoughtCo*,
      April 10, 2019, https://www.thoughtco.com/latin-american-city-struc-
      ture-1435755

31   Patrick Gillespie and Marilia Brocchetto, "This company created the
      world's biggest bribery ring," *CNN Business*, April 5, 2017, https://mon-
      ey.cnn.com/2017/04/05/news/economy/odebrecht-latin-america-cor-
      ruption/index.html

32   "Favelas as Affordable Housing," *Catalytic Communities*, https://cat-
      comm.org/vision/

33   Jennifer Paluch and Joseph Herrera, "Homeless Populations Are Rising
      around California," Public Policy Institute of California, February
      21, 2023, https://www.ppic.org/blog/homeless-populations-are-ris-
      ing-around-california/

34   Rep. Roger Williams and Michelle Steeb, "Lessons learned from a
      failed bet on 'Housing First,'" *The Hill*, November 16, 2021, https://the-
      hill.com/blogs/congress-blog/politics/581841-lessons-learned-from-a-
      failed-bet-on-housing-first/

35 Barbara Y, "Transitional Housing for Recovering Addicts," *Addiction Talk Club*, July 19, 2022, https://www.addictiontalkclub.com/transition-al-housing-for-recovering-addicts/

36 Trisha Thandi, "S.F. estimate to end street homelessness drops to $1 billion," *San Francisco Chronicle*, March 21, 2023, https://www.sfchronicle.com/sf/article/sf-homeless-crisis-shelter-housing-report-17850629.php

37 Tim Johns, "San Francisco supervisor says city's $1.45 billion budget plan to end homelessness won't work," *ABC7 San Francisco*, https://abc7news.com/sf-homeless-plan-housing-all-san-francisco-super-visor-rafael-mandelman/12760671/#:~:text=SF%20supervisor%20says%20city's%20%241.45,end%20homelessness%20won't%20work&-text=San%20Francisco%20Supervisor%20Rafael%20Mandelman,t%20solve%20the%20actual%20problem.

38 Thomas Fuller, "Why Does It Cost $750,000 to Build Affordable Housing in San Francisco?," *The New York Times*, February 20, 2020, https://www.nytimes.com/2020/02/20/us/California-housing-costs.html

39 "Los Angeles is spending up to $837,000 to house a single homeless person," *The Associated Press*, February 24, 2022, accessed via *KTLA 5*, https://ktla.com/news/los-angeles-is-spending-up-to-837000-to-house-a-single-homeless-person/

40 Josh Haskell, "Audit of LA's homelessness measure shows cost per housing unit as much as $837,000," *ABC 7 Eyewitness News Los Angeles*, February 26, 2022, https://abc7.com/prop-hhh-housing-los-angeles-audit/11600642/

41 "It's Time For Common Sense Solutions on Housing the Homeless," Matt Mahan for Mayor, https://mahanforsanjose.com/com-mon-sense-housing-homeless/

42 "City Council Adds 'Quick-Build' Housing Units To Reach 2022 Goal," *San Jose Inside,* https://www.sanjoseinside.com/news/city-coun-cil-adds-quick-build-housing-units-to-reach-2022-goal/

43 Scott Beyer, "Scott Beyer's New Years housing recommendations for new SJ Council," *Opportunity Now Silicon Valley,* January 3, 2023, https://www.opportunitynowsv.org/blog/scott-beyers-new-years-hous-ing-recommendations-for-new-sj-council

44   Manuela Tobias, "Is union labor requirement in the way of easing California's affordable housing crisis?" *The Californian*, June 18, 2021, https://www.thecalifornian.com/story/news/2021/06/18/union-labor-requirement-way-easing-californias-affordable-housing-crisis/7744589002/

45   Hannah Wiley, "In groundbreaking plan, California allows affordable housing on some commercial properties," *Los Angeles Times,* September 28, 2022, https://www.latimes.com/california/story/2022-09-28/california-affordable-housing-commercial-properties

46   Eli Wolfe, "Smaller construction projects covered under San Jose labor agreement," *San Jose Spotlight*, December 23, 2022, https://sanjosespotlight.com/san-jose-expands-coverage-of-project-labor-agreement-public-works-working-conditions/

47   "Project Labor Agreement Resource Guide," U.S. Department of Labor, Project Labor Agreement Resource Guide | U.S. Department of Labor (dol.gov)

48   Jason M. Ward, "The Effects of Project Labor Agreements on the Production of Affordable Housing," RAND, https://www.rand.org/pubs/research_reports/RRA1362-1.html.

49   "Global Americans Report: Labor Rights in the Americas," *Global Americans,* https://theglobalamericans.org/reports/labor-rights-in-the-americas/

50   "Public Contracts and Procurement Regulations in California: Introduction," Lorman, July 24, 2018, https://www.lorman.com/resources/public-contracts-and-procurement-regulations-in-california-introduction-16992

51   "Subway ridership in Mexico City remains down," *Mexico Today,* September 13, 2021, https://mexicotoday.com/2021/09/13/subway-ridership-in-mexico-city-remains-down/

52   "Mexico City," Global BRT Data, https://brtdata.org/location/latin_america/mexico/mexico_city

53   Scott Beyer, "Peseros: A Look Inside Mexico City's Private Bus Network," *Catalyst*, October 16, 2019, https://catalyst.independent.org/2019/10/16/peseros-a-look-inside-mexico-citys-private-bus-network/

54 Zoe Mendelson, "Mapping Mexico City's Vast, Informal Transit System," *Fast Company,* April 8, 2016, https://www.fastcompany.com/3058475/mapping-mexico-citys-vast-informal-transit-system

55 "The Last Ride of the Jitney," *SF Weekly,* March 9, 2016, https://www.sfweekly.com/news/the-last-ride-of-the-jitney/

56 "Private Transit Vehicle Permitting," San Francisco Municipal Transportation Agency, https://www.sfmta.com/projects/private-transit-vehicle-permitting

57 "Leap Transit," *Failory*, https://www.failory.com/cemetery/leap-transit

58 Adam Brinklow, "Private bus company Chariot going out of business," *Curbed San Francisco,* January 10, 2019, https://sf.curbed.com/2019/1/10/18177528/chariot-san-francisco-out-of-business

59 Christen Kafton, "SFMTA faces fiscal cliff," March 3, 2023, *KTVU,* https://www.ktvu.com/news/sfmta-faces-fiscal-cliff

60 Ricardo Cano, "Without state funding, S.F.'s Muni could cut up to 20 bus lines - starting this summer," *San Francisco Chronicle,* May 29, 2023, https://www.sfchronicle.com/sf/article/muni-bus-lines-18116809.php

61 Michelle Avery and Sandra Caballero, "Latin America is a mass-transit powerhouse. But it needs fine-tuning," World Economic Forum, June 27, 2019, https://www.weforum.org/agenda/2019/06/latin-america-is-a-mass-transit-powerhouse-but-it-needs-fine-tuning/

62 Patricia Yañez-Pagans, Daniel Martinez, Oscar A. Mitnik, Lynn Scholl, and Antonia Vazquez, "Urban Transport Systems in Latin America and the Caribbean: Challenges and Lessons Learned," Institute of Labor Economics,

63 Guillaume Thibault, "Latin America Shows Public Transit Isn't Everything," *Oliver Wyman Forum,* November 30, 2020, https://www.oliverwymanforum.com/mobility/2020/nov/latin-america-shows-public-transit-isnt-everything.html

64 "C40 Good Practice Guides: Curitiba - Bus Rapid Transit Modernisation," *C40 Cities,* February 2016, https://www.c40.org/case-studies/c40-good-practice-guides-curitiba-bus-rapid-transit-modernisation/

65 "Modernizing Bus Rapid Transit: Curitiba, Brazil," EBRD Green Cities Policy Tool, https://www.ebrdgreencities.com/policy-tool/modernizing-bus-rapid-transit-curitiba-brazil/

66 "Curitiba, Brazil: BRT Case Study," Transportation Research Board, https://onlinepubs.trb.org/onlinepubs/tcrp/tcrp90v1_cs/Curitiba.pdf

67 Joseph Goodman, Melissa Laube, and Judith Schwenk, "Curitiba Bus System is Model for Rapid Transit," *Reimagine,* Spring 2007, https://www.reimaginerpe.org/curitiba-bus-system

68 "TransMilenio Bus Rapid Transit System," Urban Sustainability Exchange, https://use.metropolis.org/case-studies/transmilenio-bus-rapid-transit-system. TransMilenio was established in 1999, per "TransMilenio: renewing Bogotá's transport system," Centre for Public Impact, March 30, 2016, https://www.centreforpublicimpact.org/case-study/transmilenio/

69 Scott Beyer, "Can Latin America Integrate Its Poor?," *Governing Magazine*, December 21, 2022, https://www.governing.com/community/can-latin-america-integrate-its-poor

70 Ricardo Cano, "It took 27 years and $300 million. Will S.F. Van Ness BRT improve traffic congestion?," *San Francisco Chronicle*, March 25, 2022 https://www.sfchronicle.com/sf/article/S-F-s-Van-Ness-transit-project-is-ready-after-17027218.php

71 "Van Ness Avenue: What Lies Beneath," City and County of San Francisco Civil Grand Jury, June 2021, p. 4, https://civilgrandjury.sfgov.org/2020_2021/2021%20CGJ%20Report_Van%20Ness%20Avenue%20-%20What%20Lies%20Beneath.pdf

72 "Van Ness Avenue Bus Rapid Transit (BRT) Feasibility Study," San Francisco County Transportation Authority, December 2006, https://www.sfcta.org/sites/default/files/2019-02/Van%20Ness%20BRTFeasibilityStudy_Dec_2006.pdf

73 Maryann Jones Thompson and Shelley D. Fargo, "Dreams & Delays: A Timeline of the Van Ness BRT Project," *The San Francisco Standard*, April 1st, 2022, https://sfstandard.com/transportation/van-ness-brt-bus-rapid-transit-history-timeline/

74 Ralph Vartabedien, "How California's Bullet Train Went Off the Rails," *The New York Times*, October 9, 2022 https://www.nytimes.com/2022/10/09/us/california-high-speed-rail-politics.html

75   Ricardo Cano, "S.F.'s Van Ness BRT created a ridership boom for Muni. Here's what the data shows," *San Francisco Chronicle*, November 3, 2022, https://www.sfchronicle.com/sf/article/S-F-s-Van-Ness-BRT-created-a-ridership-boom-17556984.php

76   Ricardo Cano, "One month after its debut, this is how S.F".s Van Ness BRT is performing," *San Francisco Chronicle,* April 28, 2022, https://www.sfchronicle.com/sf/article/sf-van-ness-17134051.php

77   "Geary Boulevard Improvement Project," *San Francisco Municipal Transportation Agency,* https://www.sfmta.com/projects/geary-boule-vard-improvement-project

78   Brand Studio, "The CA5 north is the best road in Central America," *La Prensa*, January 4, 2023, https://www.laprensa.hn/teinteresa/la-ca-5-norte-es-la-mejor-carretera-de-centroamerica-HH11610106

79   "Country case study: Brazil," *Public–Private Infrastructure Advisory Facility,* March 6, 2009, https://www.ppiaf.org/sites/ppiaf.org/files/documents/toolkits/highwaystoolkit-russian/6/pdf-version/brazil.pdf

80   "Brazil Toll Highways, Concessionaires and Prices," *Tollguru.com,* https://tollguru.com/toll-wiki/brazil-toll-highways-concessionaries-price

81   "South Bay Expressway," *United States Department of Transportation: Build America Bureau,* https://www.transportation.gov/buildamerica/projects/south-bay-expressway

82   "South Bay Expressway (SR 125), San Diego, CA," *United States Department of Transportation: Build America Bureau,* https://www.transportation.gov/buildamerica/projects/project-highlights/south-bay-expressway-sr-125-san-diego-ca

83   Baruch Feigenbaum, "South Bay Expressway Proves that P3s Protect Taxpayers," *Reason*, October 10, 2016, https://reason.org/commentary/south-bay-expressway-proves-that-p3s-protect-taxpayers/

84   "Paying for Tolls," *Florida's Turnpike*, https://floridasturnpike.com/tolls/

85   Joel Eisenbaum, "Are Texans paying twice for toll roads?" *Click 2 Houston*, https://www.click2houston.com/news/2016/11/08/are-texans-paying-twice-for-toll-roads/

86   Phate Zhang, "Didi's market share in Latin America approaches 50%," *CN Tech Post,* November 19, 2020, https://cntechpost.com/2020/11/19/didis-market-share-in-latin-america-approaches-50/

87   "The biggest food delivery apps are moving into Latin America," *IDG Connect,* December 30, 2019, https://www.idgconnect.com/article/3580982/the-biggest-food-delivery-apps-are-moving-into-latin-america.html

88   Mathilde Carter, "Leading countries in motorcycle ownership rate in Latin America as of 2018," *Statista,* https://www.statista.com/statistics/964866/motorbike-ownership-rate-latin-america-country/

89   Julia Buckley, "E-scooters suddenly appeared everywhere, but now they're riding into serious trouble," *CNN Travel,* November 22, 2019, https://www.cnn.com/travel/article/electric-scooter-bans-world/index.html. For instance, in November 2019, Los Angeles " suspended Uber's permit to rent e-scooters because of its failure to share ride-tracking data with the Los Angeles Department of Transportation [though other operators remained authoritzed]...[a]nd in San Francisco, the scooter companies were dubbed 'spoiled brats' by Aaron Peskin, one of the legislators who voted to clamp down on the companies when they were introduced in 2018."

90   Andrew J. Hawkins, "Revel launches its shared electric mopeds in San Francisco," *The Verge,* August 31, 2020, https://www.theverge.com/2020/8/31/21408769/revel-launch-san-francisco-electric-moped-price

91   Dan Rivoli, "Revel Mopeds Attract New Yorkers On The Go, and Lawsuits," *Spectrum News NY 1,* July 24, 2020, https://www.ny1.com/nyc/all-boroughs/transit/2020/07/24/revel-mopeds-attract-new-yorkers-on-the-go--and-lawsuits

92   Jessica, "The History of Medellin's Laureles Neighborhood," *CasaCol,* https://en.casacol.co/2022/09/09/history-medellins-laureles-neighborhood/

93   David Stieckenreiter, "Laureles Area for Living in Medellin," *Escape Artist*, https://www.escapeartist.com/blog/laureles-area-living-medellin/

94 "Medellín shows how nature-based solutions can keep people and planet cool," UN Environment Programme, July 17, 2019, https://www.unep.org/news-and-stories/story/medellin-shows-how-nature-based-solutions-can-keep-people-and-planet-cool

95 Anastasia Moloney, "Colombia's Medellin plants 'green corridors' to beat rising heat," *PreventionWeb*, July 28, 2021, https://www.preventionweb.net/news/colombias-medellin-plants-green-corridors-beat-rising-heat

96 Iyna Bort Caruso, "An Exclusive Enclave," *Sotheby's International Realty*, https://www.sothebysrealty.com/eng/destinations/leblon-rio-brazil

97 "Urban & Community Forestry Inflation Reduction Act Grants," *U.S. Forest Service*, https://www.fs.usda.gov/managing-land/urban-forests/ucf

98 "Urban Greening Program," *California Climate Investments*, https://www.caclimateinvestments.ca.gov/urban-greening

99 "New Greenspaces Help Grow Community Connectivity in Coachella," *California Climate Investments*, https://www.caclimateinvestments.ca.gov/2020-profiles/urban-greening

100 Geraldine Estevez, "Coachella receives $3.19M urban greening grant to upgrade Grapefruit Boulevard area," *Desert Sun*, November 2, 2018, https://www.desertsun.com/story/news/2018/11/02/coachella-receives-3-19-m-state-grant-urban-greening/1860673002/

101 "Sacramento," *Treepedia*, https://senseable.mit.edu/treepedia/cities/sacramento

102 Randol White, "How Did Sacramento Get So Many Trees?," *CapRadio*, December 20, 2018, https://www.capradio.org/articles/2018/12/20/how-did-sacramento-get-so-many-trees/

103 "Urban Greening Program," *California Climate Investments*, https://www.caclimateinvestments.ca.gov/urban-greening

104 Sarah Brown, "A Guide to Rio de Janeiro's Favelas," *The Culture Trip*, April 12, 2022, https://theculturetrip.com/south-america/brazil/articles/a-guide-and-history-to-rio-de-janeiros-favelas/

105 Hernando de Soto, "The Mystery of Capital: Why Capitalism Triumphs in the West and Fails Everywhere Else," 2000

106 Jennifer Paluch and Joseph Herrera, "Homeless Populations Are Rising around California," Public Policy Institute of California, February 21, 2023, https://www.ppic.org/blog/homeless-populations-are-rising-around-california/

107 Arla Bendix, "UN expert: "San Francisco's homelessness crisis is a human rights violation and suggests 'a cruelty that is unsurpassed,'" Business Insider, November 12, 2018, https://www.businessinsider.com/un-expert-san-francisco-homeless-cruelty-2018-11

108 Scott Beyer, "The Soft Tyranny of Occupational Licensing," Catalyst, July 12, 2022, https://catalyst.independent.org/2022/07/12/tyranny-occupational-licensing/

109 "Argentine capital seeks to improve iconic Villa 31 slum," The Seattle Times, May 17, 2017, https://www.seattletimes.com/nation-world/argentine-capital-seeks-to-improve-iconic-villa-31-slum/

110 Scott Beyer, "Can Latin America Integrate its Poor?," Governing Magazine, December 21, 2022, https://www.governing.com/community/can-latin-america-integrate-its-poor

111 "Skid Row Infrastructure Project Gets $47.5 Million in State Funding," City News Service, December 21, 2022, accessed via NBC Los Angeles, https://www.nbclosangeles.com/news/local/skid-row-infrastructure-project-gets-47-5-million-in-state-funding/3060360/

112 Meghan Roos, "'We Need to Take Back Our Tenderloin': SF Mayor London Breed Takes Aim at Crime Surge," Newsweek, December 14, 2021, https://www.newsweek.com/we-need-take-back-our-tenderloin-sf-mayor-london-breed-takes-aim-crime-surge-1659417

113 "Startup Cities Map," Adrianople Group, https://www.startupcitiesmap.com/map

114 Jenn Henry, "The Private City: Irvine (Company), California," University of California (Irvine) School of Law, Spring 2012, https://escholarship.org/content/qt59d8c03d/qt59d8c03d_noSplash_ade53816a-74caa76fbf86a0a87b14d4c.pdf?t=m7eza0

115 Steve Stanek and Leonard Gilroy, "Sandy Springs Incorporates, Inspires New Wave of 'Private' Cities in Georgia," Reason, November 1, 2006, https://reason.org/commentary/sandy-springs-incorporates-ins/

116 Scott Beyer, "Does Arizona's Parking-Free "Culdesac" Have a Future?," *Catalyst,* October 1, 2021, https://catalyst.independent.org/2021/10/01/parking-free-culdesac/

117 Scott Beyer, "Honduras' Charter City Experiment," *Catalyst,* January 30, 2023, https://catalyst.independent.org/2023/01/30/charter-city-experiment/

118 Gustavo Palencia, "Honduran Congress unanimously nixes special economic zones," *Reuters,* April 21, 2022, https://www.reuters.com/world/americas/honduran-congress-unanimously-nixes-special-economic-zones-2022-04-21/

119 Scott Beyer, "Startup City 2 on my cross-global tour: Cayala," *LinkedIn,* August 2022, https://www.linkedin.com/posts/market-urbanist_startup-city-2-on-my-cross-global-tour-cayala-activity-6971913894176923648-25U6/

120 "Michatoya Pacifico," https://www.michatoyapacifico.com/

121 Scott Beyer, *LinkedIn,* https://www.linkedin.com/posts/market-urbanist_one-purpose-of-my-15-year-trip-is-to-scout-activity-6970428652358402048-lzH-/

122 Scott Beyer, "How to Create an Urban Amenity Beach," *Catalyst,* March 27, 2023, https://catalyst.independent.org/2023/03/27/urban-beaches/

123 "Porte Norte," https://www.portanorte.com/

124 Shawn Hubler, "The State of California's 'State of Jefferson,'" *The New York Times, May 26, 2021,* https://www.nytimes.com/2021/05/26/us/california-jefferson-secession.html

125 Tay Wiles, "A Separatist State of Mind," *High Country News, January 22, 2018,* https://www.hcn.org/issues/50.1/communities-rural-discontent-finds-a-home-in-the-state-of-jefferson

126 Jeff Daniels, "Draper plan that would carve up California into three states qualifies for November ballot," *CNBC,* June 13, 2018, https://www.cnbc.com/2018/06/13/tim-drapers-three-californias-plan-qualifies-for-november-ballot.html

127 "State Supreme Court Blocks 3 Californias Initiative From November Ballot, *The Associated Press*, July 18, 2018, accessed via *CBS News Sacramento*, https://www.cbsnews.com/sacramento/news/ca-supreme-court-blocks-3-split/

128 Brad Haynes, Latin America's 'Pink Tide' May Have Hit Its High-Water Mark," *Reuters,* December 22, 2022, accessed via *U. S. News and World Report*, https://www.usnews.com/news/world/articles/2022-12-22/latin-americas-pink-tide-may-have-hit-its-high-water-mark

129 Chris Dalby, Parker Asmann, and Gabrielle Gorder, "Why Does Latin America Dominate the World's Most Violent Cities List?,"*InSight Crime*, March 24, 2022, https://insightcrime.org/news/latin-america-stranglehold-world-most-violent-cities-list/

130 Priscilla Alvarez, "US border encounters top 2 million in fiscal year 2022," *CNN Politics*, October 22, 2022, https://www.cnn.com/2022/10/22/politics/border-encounters-migrants-2022/index.html

131 Morgan Keith, "California has the highest poverty level of all states in the US, according to US Census Bureau data," *Business Insider,* September 14, 2021, https://www.businessinsider.com/california-has-highest-poverty-level-in-the-us-census-bureau-2021-9

About the Author

Scott Beyer owns Market Urbanist, a media company advocating for free-market city policy. He owns a spinoff consulting firm - Beyer Policy - that tries to make these reforms a political reality.

Beyer is also an urban affairs journalist who writes regular columns for Independent Institute, *Governing Magazine,* and HousingOnline.com. He freelances for other publications, and does frequent media interviews on TV, radio and podcast.

In 2017, Scott Beyer founded Market Urbanist (previously Market Urbanism Report), a media company advocating for free-market city policy reform. But before this career he began as an everyday lover of cities.

It started when, as a kid, he would visit his grandfather to tour the fancy hotels and monuments of Washington, DC. Throughout his twenties he lived in New York, San Francisco and Portland, and traveled to many other U.S. cities, working odd jobs and exploring the cities at street level. He began researching why they grew as they did, absorbing the works of Jane Jacobs, Edward Glaeser and more.

In 2015, Beyer wanted to take a deeper look into how these free-market ideas could work on grounds. Over a 3-year period, he lived in 30 cities for a month each. Throughout the trip he met countless people - developers, planners, officials, activists, and other professionals - who were doing interesting things in their cities, and profiled them in his urban affairs column for Forbes. But he also saw the structural problems, like high home prices and traffic congestion, that were hurting cities.

Market Urbanist theory struck him, even more than before he started the trip, as the best way to solve these problems. So in 2017, during the Salt Lake City stop, he launched his own Market Urbanist blog - Market Urbanist. The blog has helped grow what was already a sizable Market Urbanism movement. It's full of people who want to restore classical liberalism in cities, under the premise that this would make housing cheaper, transportation faster, and cities better-run. Scott Beyer owns Market Urbanist.

About Pacific Research Institute

The Pacific Research Institute (PRI) champions freedom, opportunity, and personal responsibility by advancing free-market policy solutions. It provides practical solutions for the policy issues that impact the daily lives of all Americans, and demonstrates why the free market is more effective than the government at providing the important results we all seek: good schools, quality health care, a clean environment, and a robust economy.

Founded in 1979 and based in San Francisco, PRI is a non-profit, non-partisan organization supported by private contributions. Its activities include publications, public events, media commentary, community leadership, legislative testimony, and academic outreach.

Center for Business and Economics

PRI shows how the entrepreneurial spirit—the engine of economic growth and opportunity—is stifled by onerous taxes, regulations, and lawsuits. It advances policy reforms that promote a robust economy, consumer choice, and innovation.

Center for Education

PRI works to restore to all parents the basic right to choose the best educational opportunities for their children. Through research and grassroots outreach, PRI promotes parental choice in education, high academic standards, teacher quality, charter schools, and school-finance reform.

Center for the Environment

PRI reveals the dramatic and long-term trend toward a cleaner, healthier environment. It also examines and promotes the essential ingredients for abundant resources and environmental quality: property rights, markets, local action, and private initiative.

Center for Health Care

PRI demonstrates why a single-payer Canadian model would be detrimental to the health care of all Americans. It proposes market-based reforms that would improve affordability, access, quality, and consumer choice.

Center for California Reform

The Center for California Reform seeks to reinvigorate California's entrepreneurial self-reliant traditions. It champions solutions in education, business, and the environment that work to advance prosperity and opportunity for all the state's residents.

Center for Medical Economics and Innovation

The Center for Medical Economics and Innovation aims to educate policymakers, regulators, health care professionals, the media, and the public on the critical role that new technologies play in improving health and accelerating economic growth.

Free Cities Center

The Free Cities Center cultivates innovative ideas to improve our cities and urban life based around freedom and property rights – not government.